table of contents

from the staff

One of the easiest ways to change the look and feel of a room is to focus on the windows. For the biggest "wow" factor, use custom window treatments designed specifically for your room. Don't worry—expert sewing skills are not necessary to fashion personalized panels, shades, and valances. We've assembled a collection of easy-to-sew masterpieces that are sure to enliven your decorating scheme. Turn the pages for inspiring ideas, flip to the back for step-by-step instructions, and then prepare to amaze yourself—and your friends—with your curtain-making skills!

fabric 101

Fabulous window treatments start with great fabrics. With such a wide array of options available, it can be a challenge to winnow the choices down to one. This crash course in classic fabric fundamentals—along with our picks for the best weaves for windows—will help you make a smart selection.

COTTON is durable, strong, and affordable. This versatile fiber dyes easily, blends well with other fabrics, and can be woven into a wide range of patterns, colors, weights, and textures. It also accepts applications that make it resistant to flame, water, stains, and shrinking. It's machine-washable, but cotton wrinkles and may eventually yellow or fade in the sun. Weight affects how cotton fabric drapes; higher thread counts wear better.

LINEN is a strong, smooth, and sophisticated fabric. More expensive than cotton, linen tends to be stiff when draping and it wrinkles easily. Sunlight can weaken its natural fibers; extend its life with linings and interlinings. Most linen is dry-clean only. Crisp and clean, linen is a popular choice for traditional rooms; however, its uneven fibers and organic grace also make it a lovely window choice for casual settings.

SILK is a costly and lustrous fabric that makes soft and graceful window dressings. It drapes beautifully and absorbs dye well, making the colors bright and clear. However, sun can fade or weaken silk, so line and interline silk treatments and block the sun with shades or blinds. Unless treated, water will spot silk. Designer silks require dry cleaning.

WOOL is long-wearing, moderately priced, and hangs in full, loose folds, making it perfect for long draperies. The fibers, when woven, have a spiral shape that creates air pockets that serve as insulation against winter chills and summer sun. Unless chemically treated, wool attracts moths and weakens over time when in direct sunlight. Wool must be dry cleaned.

MAN-MADE fibers are appreciated for their drape and easy care. Classics include nylon, rayon, and polyester. Although they are stronger than their natural counterparts, synthetics may pill and are typically not as attractive as natural fibers. Look for blends that contain at least 20 percent natural fibers; synthetics boost a natural fiber's strength, longevity, and wrinkle resistance.

WINNING WEAVES

Chambray: This lightweight cotton fabric works particularly well for flat panels and poufy treatments in casual settings.

Chenille: This caterpillarlike fabric hangs beautifully as a panel; add a lining for volume.

Chintz: Its light weight makes it an excellent choice for treatments with ruffles and poufs.

Damask: A heavy fabric, damask works well for covered cornices, Roman shades, and panels.

Moiré: Its shimmering finish looks best in formal settings; use it for flat panels or poufed treatments.

Sheer: This fluid, see-through fabric gently diffuses light. Pair it with shades or blinds for privacy.

Taffeta: A stiff fabric that retains its shape well, taffeta makes full-bodied draperies.

Twill: Tightly woven and full bodied, twill works well for windowsill- or floor-length panels but doesn't puddle nicely.

Velvet: An elegant fabric that works well for formal treatments, velvet blocks drafts and light effectively.

THE LOWDOWN ON LININGS

The hallmark of a fine drapery is its lining, which gives weight to a treatment and protects the fabric from sunlight. For lining material, pure cotton sateen is the most widely available. Reline draperies as needed to protect the fabric.

no-sew, low-sew
TREATMENTS

Not an expert seamstress? No problem. Solve your window decorating dilemmas with these beginner-friendly curtains and valances.

Paper chase

Keep it simple with no-sew paper café curtains, *below* and *right*. Drape sturdy decorative paper (available at art-supply stores) over a rod. Pinch a row of pleats a few inches beneath the fold and pierce each with a hole punch. Tie the pleats with lengths of narrow ribbon.

Kraft-y creation

Top off natural bamboo shades with kraft paper cornices, *left*. Cut a length of kraft paper the width of the window frame plus 20 inches. Fold the paper in half lengthwise, making a sharp crease. Fold a box pleat at the center of the paper length, *below*. Staple the top of the paper to a 1×2 board, creating a pleat at each end of the board; hang the treatment above the window using L-brackets.

Heirloom design

Convert a dresser scarf into a charming kitchen window treatment, *top* and *above*. Search antiques shops for decorative linens, or ask Grandma for an heirloom piece. Simply drape the fabric over a basic tension rod.

Tack it on

Dressing a window doesn't have to be complicated. Take a cue from this fabric designer's studio, *left*. The valance is a fabric remnant, finished around the edges with fusible web and tacked to the top of the window frame. A similar sheer panel hangs below on a tension rod that fits inside the window frame. A row of starfish, secured to the panel with glue, dances across the window at sash height.

panels

Whether they run floor to ceiling or simply fit the window frame, panels are a classic choice. Even beginners can make custom treatments that suit their taste and decor. Read through our basic instructions and then get creative with fabric colors and patterns. Add embellishments to give the panels personality.

flat panels

Give every window a beautiful view with custom panels that suit your style. The easiest solution is a flat panel, which is a length of fabric hemmed on all four sides. Let these ideas for embellishing a basic flat panel inspire you. Then turn to page 42 for instructions.

Fun with finials

Dress up flat panels by hanging them from interesting hardware. These chocolate-and-cream windowpane-check draperies *below* and at *right* hang from brown finials that pop crisply against the striped walls. The contrast of light and dark invigorates and adds verve to the room.

Banded beauty

Make your guests green with envy with simple elegant window panels. With its embroidered leaf motif, this drapery fabric *above* is a contemporary update on a traditional floral. A wide band of green fabric at the top continues the line of the green stripe painted at the same height on the adjacent wall. The panels are hung from brushed-nickel curtain rings, *left*, which were stitched onto the green fabric band.

flat panels

Not just for naps

Consider flat sheets for a no-stress window solution. Available in an array of prints and solids, they're already hemmed. Transform a vine pattern into a crisp, elegant panel, *right*, with a border of 1-inch satin ribbon. Stitch it on or attach it with iron-on hem tape. Space ½-inch grommets 6 inches apart along the top of the panel; then slip it onto a slim rod.

Go for grommets

Opt for cool, clean-lined window coverings in modern spaces. Flat panels hung from large grommets, *left* and *below*, are a fuss-free solution. The funky fabric in vibrating shades of blue and green adds pattern and movement to the colorful space. In a minimalist setting, try a similar treatment using a neutral fabric with interesting texture.

Hooked on style

Top off a series of French doors with simple linen valances, *right*. Because a decorative rod might weigh down the look, the valances are suspended from modest hooks screwed into the wall close to the ceiling, *below*. Their placement also makes it easy to open the doors without having the fabric get in the way.

Higher elevation

Create a dramatic entrance by hanging draperies a foot or more above the top of a doorway and allowing the panels to puddle on the floor. These platinum-color semisheer linen-and-spun-rayon panels at *right* hang from decorative brass L-hooks. Simple brass rings, hand-sewn along the top of the curtain panels, attach the panels to the hooks.

pocket panels

A pocket is the quickest way to attach a drapery panel to a rod, which simply slips through a channel sewn into the panel's top edge. Pockets are so easy to work with, you'll have time to get creative. For instructions, turn to page 42.

Fabric trio

Trick guests into believing you're an expert seamstress with these triple-treat draperies at *right*. They're actually pocket panels with lining and banding in two coordinating fabrics. When the panels flip up, covered buttons hold the revealing look in place.

On the edge

Give your little girl a window treatment that's as cute and sassy as she is. Fashioned from pink gingham and yards of embroidered ribbon, these simple panels look like they came straight from a high-end home decor catalog. Hem the edges of a standard pocket panel, then topstitch rows of pretty ribbon along the bottom for a custom creation she'll love.

pocket panels

Trim treatment

Enliven a casement window with pocket panels sized to fit the panes, *right*. The slim treatment allows the window to open for ventilation with a degree of privacy. The blue stripes look tailored, while the beaded trim adds a light-hearted touch.

Sheer sizzle

Punch up a barely-there curtain with this colorful treatment, *below*. The base is a sheer pocket panel covered with crinkle-texture fabric strips. The strips are stitched with overlapping seams to create a border between colors.

Finishing touches

Welcome Baby home with a room filled with darling details. This room's sweet curtain valance at *left* and *below* is simply a shortened pocket panel featuring three bands of coordinating fabric and kid-friendly embellishments, including pom-pom and rickrack trims.

Short and simple

Dress a window fashionably without full-length attire using charming café curtains, *opposite, bottom right*. The popular treatment provides privacy with a view. While they typically cover the bottom half of a window and are paired with a valance, where they stop and start is your choice. Hem the curtains to stop just above the sill so the panels don't flare outward; then hang them with a curtain or tension rod.

tab-top panels

Unpretentious and fuss-free, tab-top curtains offer the perfect foundation for getting more creative with a basic window treatment. Tabs are simply loops of fabric sewn into the panel's top seam. For instructions, turn to page 42.

Fit to be tied
Soften a window while filtering light with an embroidered sheer, *left* and *below*. For more texture and depth, partner the sheers with simple gingham panels. Fasten both sets of panels to the rod with casual ties at the top.

Thin is in

Accentuate a wall of 12-foot-tall windows with half-width panels, *above*, that are purely decorative. They soften the more functional plantation shutters. Constructed of three patterns—plaid, floral, and gingham—in different scales, the tabbed panels are hung from wooden finials, *right*, mounted between each set of windows.

tab-top panels

Tailored treatment

Bring dressmaker detailing to simple tab-top panels, *right*.
Apply a border of grosgrain ribbon to each panel's sides and
lower edge. Dot the top with distnction by adding a button to
the base of each tab.

Band together

Combine classic fabrics, such as toile and plaid, in
a French country-inspired treatment, *below*. Flaring as they
reach the floor, the panels are feminine and elegant. Bands of
plaid slip over the tab tops for a unique and tailored look,
below right.

Bathed in beauty

Convert shower curtains already fitted with grommets into interesting window treatments. Paired with woven blinds, these Capri-length panels at *right* and *below* are tied to a rod with ribbon to create a relaxed look in this living room.

Clothes line

Add summer-on-the-farm style to country or cottage decor with a buckled-up window treatment, *right*. Simply hand-stitch a row of buckles designed for overalls along the top of each panel.

pleated panels

Classically tailored, pleated curtains generally add a traditional look to a decorating scheme. For a more casual or contemporary look, however, choose modern fabrics and simple rods. For basic instructions, turn to page 42.

On the border

Hanging higher and wider than the window trim, these vibrant yellow pinch-pleat panels, *above*, give the windows more prominence. Plaid fabric cut on the bias bands the panels, which are lined with flannel to make them appear fuller.

Tied in a bow

Splurge on luxurious silk ribbons to elevate the look of pinch-pleat draperies, *above*. Here, the bottom of each panel is enhanced with topstitched ivory and chocolate-brown ribbons, and the top is dressed up with petite ribbon bows at the base of each pinch pleat, *above right*.

Stripe it rich

Highlight dramatic windows with bold striped panels, *above*. Hung at intervals along a curved brass rod, the panels are made of three complementary shades of heavy silk taffeta sewn together in horizontal bands. The lengthy curtains soften the windows without blocking light and set the tone for a comfortable space.

pleated panels

On the ball

Define windows without detracting from the light and view with a pretty valance. This simple goblet-pleat window topper at *right* and *below* is made of rustic gingham and finished with ball fringe.

Big band

Flank simple striped shades with full-length panels for a luxe look, *left.* Pressed pleats create clean lines at the tops of the panels, *below,* but give way to soft folds when they reach the floor, *below left.* Woven-texture caramel trim adds rich detail to the no-frills panels.

shades
&
valances

Even the simplest window treatment can transform a room. Add function and fun with a Roman shade, create a waterfall effect with a swag, or show off a view with a valance. Learn the basics with our easy instructions and then customize the look with pretty fabrics and eye-catching trims.

roman shades

Whether they are made to fit within a window or just beyond the frame's edge, Roman shades need not be strictly utilitarian. Dress up the tailored treatment with complementary fabrics and trims. For instructions, see page 42.

Center of attention

Make pattern-heavy Roman shades, *above*, the focal point in a room that has white walls and a neutral color palette. Made of a thin cotton that creates a sharp pleat (choose heavier fabrics for softer pleats), the shades are trimmed with a row of gold tassels.

Easy elegance

Dress down a formal room with a casual Roman shade, *above*. The simple treatment, which offers privacy and light control, is a fuss-free alternative to heavy draperies. To make a Roman shade feel at home in classic surroundings, choose a rich fabric and embellish the treatment with a border of velvety scallop-edge ribbon, *left*.

window treatments **27**

roman shades

Mix and match

Enliven a monochromatic shade, such as this lotus pattern treatment *above* and at *right* with a lively striped valance. A Roman shade is a lovely way to dress up a standard frame or underscore a clerestory. If you have a wide window, choose a lightweight fabric for ease in raising the shade.

Pattern play

Show off finely patterned fabrics with a Roman shade. A checkerboard floral-and-greenery motif elevates the simple shade *above* from plain to work of art. A scalloped bottom edge adds another designer touch, *top*.

Tie one on

Highlight casual cottage decor with light and airy cotton shades, *above*. Floral fabric ties, cut from the same fabric as the pillows, give the fresh-as-a-summer-breeze Roman shades a custom look. When the ties are removed, the shades drop for more privacy and light control.

roman shades

Triple treat

Provide a contemporary counterpoint to the country style of a youthful bedroom with a trio of red-and-white Roman shades, *above*. Made of a weighty colorful cotton fabric and accented with precise banding, the tailored shades are mounted inside the window frame to show off the painted-wood trim.

Bottoms up

Give a simple Roman shade a designer look with custom details. Purchase a tab-top valance as wide as your Roman shade and cut it into strips. Use the tabbed top to accent the bottom edge of the shade and trim the sides with the remaining fabric. On the back of the shade, untie the cords from the bottom rings and retie them to the adjacent rings so the bottom edge will show.

swags

Take the stark edge off a bare window or add another layer to an opulent treatment with a simple swag. The easiest treatments to create, swags can be left bare or embellished for more pizzazz. For instructions, see page 42.

Light and airy

Make the most of your home's architectural details by keeping window coverings to a minimum. The loosely hung lacy swag *below* adds softness to the window without concealing the decorative moldings. An in-frame shade ensures privacy.

Formal wear

Allow light to flood an upstairs hallway with a luxurious treatment, *above,* that is sophisticated in its simplicity. Upholstery-weight velvet backed with raw silk collapses into rich folds that hang from a fabric-covered rod capped with decorative copper finials.

Cover-up

Add depth and interest to a swag by dressing up the rod from which it hangs. The feminine treatment *above* is attached with hook-and-loop tape to a dowel covered in the same plaid fabric that edges the swag.

Softer side

Use a simple swag to complement another treatment for a hard-edge window. Here, a swag made of red-and-white cotton ticking, *above right* and *right,* enhances and softens the look of red shutters on this kitchen window.

box pleats

The strong lines and traditional appeal of a box-pleat valance make it a natural choice for a room with a formal air. The stationary treatment's crisply stitched pleats lie flat against a mounting board. For instructions, see page 42.

Show-off

Emphasize a valance's linear look with high-contrast banding along the edges. Ribbon with a Greek key pattern trims the bottom of this valance *above* and is folded into rosettes that are stitched to the top of each pleat. When using striped fabric for a box-pleat valance, plan the pleats so they align with the stripes to reinforce the pattern's geometry.

Simply chic

Give a box-pleat valance a dignified look by using a tone-on-tone floral print and adding pleat-and-button detailing. Combined with matching side panels, the valance elegantly frames the window.

box pleats

Peek-a-boo

Lighten up the look of sophisticated box pleats by using playful or colorful fabrics, such as this checkerboard-blue cotton at *right*. Having a companion fabric, such as this vibrant yellow *below*, peek through the pleat emphasizes the construction and picks up on a room's accent color.

Quiet beauty

Add some frills to a large valance by running inverted pleats along the full length of the treatment, *left* and *below left*, and then pair it with full panels. Using the same neutral floral fabric on the entire treatment gives it a cohesive look that's textural and lush but not overpowering.

Smooth as silk

Construct simple pleated valances from luxurious raw silk, *above*, for a sparse but stylish look. Pinch-pleat draperies in the same warm camel color solidify the look—complementing rather than competing with the room's gallery-inspired atmosphere.

finishing touches

A colorful necklace can turn an ordinary black dress into something unforgettable. A beautiful tieback can do the same for a window treatment. When it comes to dressing windows, pay attention to details. Even a simple treatment deserves a special flourish.

1. Embellish a standard fabric tieback with a pretty bauble. This thick cuff, fashioned from a double-folded strip of velvet, gets extra pizzazz from a beaded tassel.

2. Make lush tiebacks from millinery flowers—originally intended for ladies' hats. Sew or glue the blossoms, available at fabrics and crafts stores, to a length of ribbon or cording, and pull the panels back so the flowers rest at the inside edges.

3. Blur the line between the indoors and outdoors with a whimsical floral tieback. Simply twist lengths of wire-stem flowers and greenery around the panel.

4. Give your window the glam treatment it deserves with a large tassel attached to braided roping. Ball-fringe trim sewn along the edge of the panel is another elegant touch.

5. Simplify your curtains with a no-fuss tieback. Made from a finial attached to a rod, this easy solution is a slick, contemporary alternative to showier adornments.

6. Add instant drama to a window with a wide tieback made from contrasting fabric and edged with fringe. Here, the same fringe and coordinating silk were used to band the inside edge of the panel.

7. Bring new meaning to curtain jewelry with tiebacks fashioned from jeweled accessories. Use a vintage bracelet to cinch a panel gathered at the center of a window.

8. Use found objects to give your curtains individual character. Sheer ribbons tied onto an oversize paper clip adorn this breezy tieback panel. Achieve a similar look by using ribbons tied to copper wire.

TRIM TUTORIAL

Fabrics and crafts stores offer a dizzying array of embellishments you can use to create tiebacks. Beads, shells, buttons, leather, feathers, appliqués, pom-poms, and embroidered tapes add texture, movement, and sparkle to your windows.

drapery basics

Rings and Things

These helpful accessories can make quick work of making draperies. This is your guide to basic drapery hardware and notions.

1. Plastic Rings: Use these rings when making Roman shades, café curtains, and tieback hooks. Pictured left to right: 1-inch-, ¾-inch-, and ½-inch-diameter rings.

2. Slip-In Hook: This 3x1-inch-long hook is used with pinch-pleated draperies that are not sewn closed at the bottom of the heading. The looped end of this drapery hook slips into a pleat, leaving the hook on the outside of the fabric.

3. Pin-On Hook: Best used for heavyweight fabrics, this round hook pins onto the back of the heading. An extra-large shank allows the hook to slide smoothly over round or flat rods. Also often used with traverse rods.

4. Gold Tieback Hook: Loop a ring-fastened tieback or a curtain over this hook to secure it in place. Best used for stationary items. Other finishes are available.

5. Screw Eye: Use this screw to guide cords along a window frame or along a wooden header when making Roman shades.

6. Clear Cord Cleat: Secure curtain cords by winding them around this transparent device that screws into the wall or window frame. Other finishes are available.

7. Leaded-Weight Tape: Sew this ⅛-inch-wide length of lead into the bottom hem of draperies, sheers, and blinds to help prevent billowing of the fabric.

8. Drapery Weights: Sew this covered weight into the bottom corner of a hem to keep a window treatment from billowing.

No-Fuss Tapes

Say good-bye to the hassle of hand-gathering pleats—use gathering and pleating tapes to speed up the job. Attach the tapes with a few rows of straight stitches, then pull the cords at the ends to gather the drapery header into uniform pleats or gathers.

1. White 3½-inch Goblet Pleat Tape, 2½:1 Fullness: This tape makes pleats that resemble footed goblets.

2. Pinch-Pleat Tape, 2½:1 Fullness: A popular choice for draperies, the resulting pleats appear to be pinched together.

3. 1¼-inch Mini Pleat Tape, 2½:1 Fullness: This tape makes smaller pleats that are similar to regular pinch pleats.

4. White 1½-inch Roman Shade Tape: Rather than attach vertical rows of rings to the back of a Roman shade, sew this two-layer tape across the back in horizontal rows and slip in dowels.

5. White 1-inch Two-Cord Shirring Tape: Use this tape to make tight, closely spaced gathers along the header.

Rings and Things

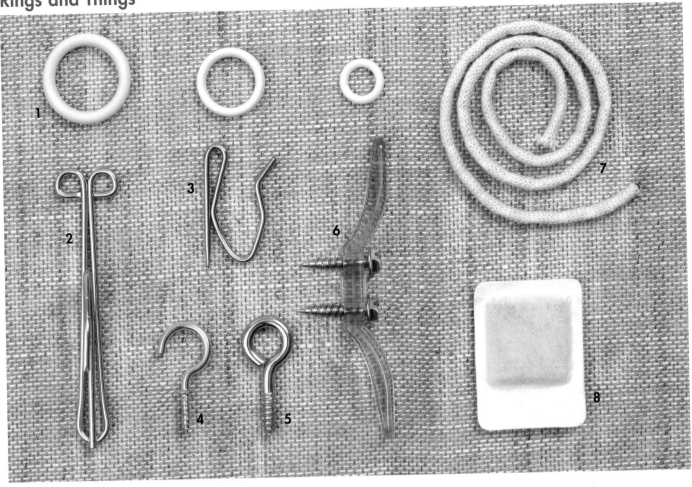

No-Fuss Tapes

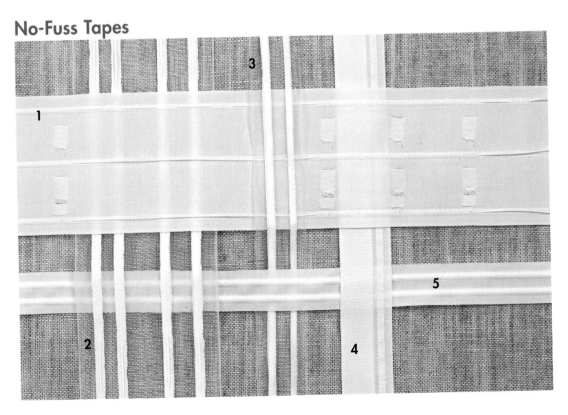

instructions

Create magnificent window treatments with this simple step-by-step guide. Use these instructions as a guideline; for custom-fit treatments, measure your windows and make adjustments to the dimensions provided as needed.

MEASURING YOUR WINDOWS

The key to sewing window treatments is learning how to measure your windows accurately. Just as pants of the right length can make an outfit look chic, window treatments must fit well to be an asset to your room. Use the illustration, *right*, to learn the basics of measuring windows.

You have two options when hanging window treatments, whether panels, blinds, shutters, or shades: inside mount (leaving the window frame visible) or outside mount (covering the frame). Regardless of where you want your new window treatments to hang, use a steel measuring tape or yardstick—neither of which will sag—to ensure accurate measurements.

Inside Mount

Measure the opening width at the top, middle, and bottom of the window (inside the frame); record the narrowest measurement. Measure the length of the window at the left, middle, and right, from the top to the sill; record the longest measurement. Round your measurements to the closest ⅛ inch.

Outside Mount

Measure the window width (including the frame) and add at least 3 inches to each side of the opening (if wall space allows) to completely cover the window frame. Measure the window length (including the frame) and add at least 2 inches in height for hardware and any overlap.

Note: Mounting window treatments above the window frame can visually heighten a room.

After you decide where you are going to mount a window treatment, determine the length of the treatment. To measure the drop for draperies and curtains, measure from where you intend to install the rod to where you want the panels to fall.

To calculate the amount of fabric you'll need for a single fabric piece, measure the distance from the bottom of the drapery ring or the top of the rod to the desired length of the scarf. Add 10 inches if you want the fabric to puddle on the floor. *Note: These directions are based on using 54-inch wide fabric. Measure the width of the area to be covered. If the width for a single panel is more than 54 inches, adjust the amount of fabric yardage needed accordingly.*

Consider the style of the room when choosing an appropriate drapery or scarf length. For example, long, flowing panels will look better in a formal living room than in a bistro-style kitchen. Also, who uses the room can influence length. Keep in mind that pets may find panels that puddle on the floor a great place to curl up for a nap.

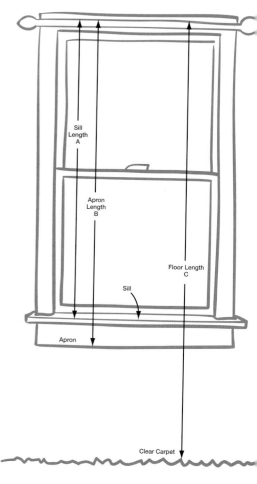

Café curtains usually break at the sill (Sill Length A); some country-style curtains may break at or below the apron (Apron Length B). Note also that floor length refers to the measurement from the top of the window or above the window trim to the floor.

FLAT PANEL

Materials

Tape measure
54-inch-wide decorator fabric
54-inch-wide contrasting decorator
  fabric for lining
Scissors
Sewing machine or needle
Thread
Iron and ironing board
Clip rings

Step by Step

1. For the width of each panel, measure the window width and halve this figure; then add 1 inch. Determine the desired length for the panel, measuring from the top of the rod to the floor, and add 10 inches.

2. Trim the selvages off the fabrics and cut curtain fabric and lining to the size determined in Step 1. If you are using a patterned fabric, be sure each piece of the curtain fabric starts at the same point in the repeat.

3. With right sides together and using a ½-inch seam allowance, stitch the panel and lining fabrics together along the side edges. Press the seams open. Stitch the top edge. Press the seam open. Stitch the bottom edge, leaving an opening in the seam large enough to turn the curtain right side out. Press the seam open.

4. Turn the curtain to the right side. Turn the seam allowances at the opening to the inside. Press flat. Hand-stitch the opening closed.

5. At each top corner, catch the edge of the curtain in a clip ring. Evenly space the remaining clips between the corners (5 clips per curtain). Hang the rings from a rod or decorative knobs.

POCKET PANEL

Materials

Tape measure
54-inch-wide decorator fabric
Lining fabric
Scissors
Sewing machine or needle
Thread
Iron and ironing board
Curtain rod

Step by Step

1. Determine the measurements of each panel. Each panel should be as wide as the window (for fuller panels, multiply the width of the window by 1½ or 2), plus 4 inches for seam allowances. For the height, measure from the top of the rod to the floor; add 2 inches for seam allowances and enough additional fabric to accommodate the curtain rod. To figure the size of the pocket, follow this formula: Measure the diameter of the rod, add ¾ inch, and divide by 2. For example, for a 6-inch-diameter rod: 6 inches + ¾ inch divided by 2 = 3⅜-inch casing.

2. Trim the selvages off the curtain and lining fabrics and cut to the measurements above.

3. To hem the sides of the panel, turn under 1 inch, press, turn under another 1 inch, and press. Pin in place; stitch.

4. To make the rod casing, turn the top edge under ½ inch and press. Then turn the same edge under the necessary width to accommodate the rod (see Step 1). Press in place, pin, and stitch.

5. Hang the panel. Turn under the bottom hem to the desired length; pin. Remove the curtain from the rod. Press the fold. Turn under the raw edge to meet the crease. Press. Hemstitch the folded edge to finish the curtain.

TAB-TOP PANEL

Make sure the tabs will slide easily if the curtain is to be pulled back. The measurements given here will make 4-inch-long tabs. For larger-diameter rods, measure the diameter of the rod and allow 1 inch between the rod and panel or valance. Adjust the measurements accordingly.

Materials

Tape measure
54-inch-wide decorator fabric
Scissors
Pins
Iron and ironing board
Sewing machine or needle
Thread
Spring-tension rod or drapery rod
  with finials and mounting hardware

Step by Step

These instructions are for unlined panels. The tabs are stitched into the seam between the curtain front and the curtain facing.

1. To determine the width of a panel, tmultiply the window width by 1½ and add 2 inches for seam allowances. Determine the desired length and add 1 inch for seams.
Note: The tabs will drop the panels approximately 2 to 2½ inches so include that in your calculations for length. If you will mount the panels or valance on a drapery rod, you may also want to add moldings into the measurements. For a fuller look, double the width.

2. Trim the selvages from the curtain panel fabric. Cut the panel fabric to the measurements above. Also cut a curtain facing that is the same width as the panel and 4 inches long.

instructions

3. On the long side edges of the curtain panel, turn under ½ inch and press; then turn under ½ inch, pin, and stitch the hem in place.

4. Determine the number of tabs. Plan for one at each end and one in the center. Then divide the remaining space into even increments, about 6 inches apart, and mark with a pin where each additional tab will go on the panel fabric.

5. Following the manufacturer's instructions, fuse interfacing to the wrong side of the tab fabric. For 2-inch tabs, cut 2½-inch-wide strips into 6-inch lengths.

6. With right sides together, fold each tab in half lengthwise and stitch along the long raw edge using a ¼-inch seam allowance. Press seam open. Turn tab right side out and press it so the seam falls at the center back of the strip. When all tabs are complete, fold each in half widthwise, matching raw edges and center back seams.

7. Lay the curtain panel right side up and pin the tabs along the top edge so the center of one tab falls at each mark and the raw edges align. Using a ½-inch seam allowance, baste the tabs in place.

8. Insert the curtain rod through the tabs. Hang the curtain to check the length of the tabs. If the top of the curtain hangs too low, you can shorten the tabs at this time.

9. Finish one long edge of the curtain facing with a row of zigzag stitches. Align the curtain and facing fabrics with right sides and upper raw edges together, encasing the tabs between the two fabrics. Turn back the facing ends so they don't extend beyond the side edges of the front. Press the folds.

10. Using a ½-inch seam allowance, stitch the facing to the curtain front. Turn the facing to the wrong side of the curtain front, allowing tabs to pop up. Press. Topstitch or hand-stitch the ends of the facing to the hemmed edges of the curtain.

11. Hang the curtain. Turn under the bottom hem to the desired length and pin. Remove the curtain from the rod and press the fold. Turn under the raw edge to meet the crease; press. Hemstich the folded edge.

PINCH-PLEATED PANEL

Materials
54-inch-wide decorator fabric
Scissors
Pleating tape (for more information, see Drapery Basics, page 40)
Sewing machine and thread
Iron and ironing board

Step by Step
1. To determine the amount of tape needed, measure the curtain rod for the width required, depending on the manufacturer's instructions.

2. Figure the required width of fabric needed. Cut the curtain fabric 5 inches wider than the pleating-tape length for side hems. Add 4 to 8 inches for the bottom hem and add 2 inches at the top. (If a standard double-turned hem is 4 inches wide, the hem allowance will be 8 inches.)

3. Double-hem the sides of the curtain by first turning under 1¼ inches, pressing, turning under another 1¼ inches, and stitching. The appropriate width of the side hems will depend on the type of fabric used and the overall size of the curtain.

4. At the top of the curtain, turn under 2 inches toward the wrong side of the fabric. Line up fabric pattern details, if needed, and press. Pin the heading tape to the wrong side of the curtain, fold the ends of the heading tape under, and pin the cords out of the way. Stitch across the top and bottom of the tape, going in the same direction each time, so the tape lays flat.

5. To measure for the hem, lay the curtain on a large flat surface. Measure from the top of the curtain to the bottom, and mark the desired length with tailor's chalk. Adjust the length to accommodate the curtain rings. To make the hem, fold up the bottom fabric edge in a double-turned hem, press, and stitch in place.

6. Tie off one end of the drawstrings. Grasp the free end of the drawstrings and pull the strings to pleat the tape. Tie off the drawstrings.

7. To hang the curtain, attach clip rings to the top of the pinch pleats.

ROMAN SHADE

Materials
54-inch-wide decorator fabric
Lining fabric
Sewing machine and matching thread
Yardstick
Fabric pen
Tracing paper
Straight pins, needle
¼-inch-diameter dowel rods
Small plastic rings
2×1 board
Screw eyes
Cording
Cord pull
L-brackets
Small awning cleat

Step by Step

1. Determine the finished width and height of the shade. If the shade will be mounted inside the window frame, subtract 3/8 inch from the width so the shade can move freely.

2. Cut the fabric 3 inches longer and 3 inches wider than the finished shade size. If the needed shade is wider than the fabric, sew two fabric lengths together, matching patterns as needed, to achieve the desired width.

3. Based on the fabric design and the look desired when the shade is drawn up, determine how many folds (and thus dowel casings) will be needed. *Note: The spaces between the dowel casings (called pockets) should be the same depth, ranging from 8 to 14 inches; these instructions are for 9-inch-deep pockets. To allow the scalloped bottom edge on our shade, the second pocket up from the bottom is only 4½ inches deep—one-half the depth of all other pockets, including the bottom one.*

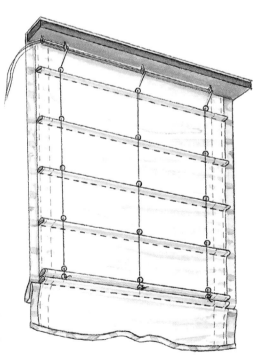

Diagram 1

4. For lining, add 3 inches, plus 1¼ inches for each dowel casing, to the finished shade length; add 1½ inches to the finished shade width. Cut to size.

5. Mark dowel casings on the lining fabric by measuring 9 inches (or desired pocket depth) up from the bottom edge; draw a horizontal line across the width of the pieces with the fabric pen. Measure 1¼ inches up from the first line (for dowel casing); draw another horizontal line. Continue measuring and drawing horizontal lines at 9 inches (pocket depth) and 1¼ inches above that to the top of the lining.

6. Turn under 1½ inches on each long side of the lining piece; machine-stitch to secure the hems. To form the bottom dowel casing, fold the lining piece with wrong sides together and match the first two horizontal lines. Pin; sew along the line. Form the remaining dowel casings in the same manner, matching and sewing each set of 1¼-inch-deep horizontal lines (see *Diagram 1*).

7. On the shade fabric, turn under 1½ inches on each long side; press hems.

8. Working on a large flat surface, lay the shade fabric piece right side down. Position the lining piece, dowel-pocket side up, on the shade piece so the bottom edges match and the lining is centered between the shade fabric's side edges. Pin in place, making sure the dowel casings are perfectly horizontal on the fabric. Machine-stitch the long side edges together along the folded edge of the lining, starting and stopping on either side of each dowel casing, making sure not to sew the edges of the dowel openings shut. Then machine-stitch

Diagram 2

through all layers along each dowel casing's horizontal stitching.

9. Draw a scallop pattern on a piece of tracing paper slightly wider than the finished shade; cut out. Position the pattern on the lining side of the shade along the bottom edge; trace. Cut both fabric layers along the scallop design; baste the cut edges together.

10. Cut a 1-inch-wide bias strip from extra decorator fabric the length of the scalloped edge plus 1 inch.

11. With right sides together, position and pin the bias strip on the decorator-fabric side of the shade along the scallop edge. Line up the raw edges and leave ½ inch on each end of the bias-strip fabric overlapping each side of the shade. Machine-stitch along the scallop ¼ inch from the raw edges. Turn under the bias-strip short ends ½ inch. Turn under the long edge of the bias strip ¼ inch; press. Fold and press the long edge of the bias strip at the stitching line over the raw scallop edge to the lining side of the shade (see *Diagram 2*); hand-stitch in place, easing the fabric as needed.

12. Turn under the top, raw edge of the shade 1 inch toward the lining side; machine-stitch to secure. Cut a dowel for each dowel casing 1 inch shorter than the casing. Insert dowels into casings; slip-stitch casings closed.

instructions

13. Lay the shade on a flat surface with the lining side up. Measure and mark ring positions on dowel casings in the following manner: Position a ring 4 inches in from each side edge of the shade on each casing. Then, evenly space rings along each casing approximately 10 to 12 inches apart. It is critical to position rings in perfect vertical columns to ensure that the shade draws up evenly. Sew rings to the middles of the dowel casings.

14. To make batten, cut 2×1 board as long as the width of the finished shade. Position the top of the shade on the 2-inch surface of the batten with the lining facing the wood and edges aligned; staple to secure. Turn the batten over so the fabric-covered surface is down. Attach screw eyes into the underside of the batten in line with the rows of rings sewn onto the casings. Determine which side of the shade the strings will draw. Attach another screw eye 1 inch in from the edge of the batten on this side.

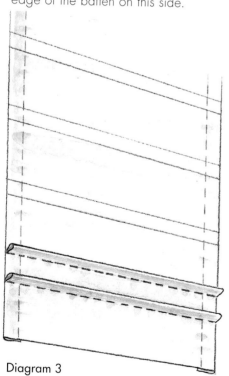

Diagram 3

15. Tie one end of one cord length to a ring on the bottom dowel casing. Thread it vertically up the shade through the corresponding rings and the corresponding screw eye on the batten. Continue threading the cord through adjacent screw eyes across the batten to draw the side of the shade. Repeat for the remaining cord lengths and remaining vertical columns of rings (see *Diagram 3*).

16. Pull the cords simultaneously taut to raise the shade, making sure the folds are even and straight. Release the shade, holding the cords together firmly. Attach the cord pull to the cords about 20 inches down; trim excess cord.

17. Mount the batten with L-brackets. Attach an awning cleat to the wall or window frame on the cord-pull side. When the shade is pulled up, secure the cords to the cleat to hold it in place.

SWAG

Materials
1×2 pine mounting board
 (see Step 1 for length)
54-inch-wide decorator fabric
Measuring tape
Table saw (optional)
Scissors
Fusible hem tape
Iron and ironing board
Staple gun and staples
Screws
Screwdriver

Step by Step
1. To determine the length of the mounting board, measure the width of the window, including the trim; subtract about 6 inches total to accommodate the knots in the valance. Cut the 1×2 pine mounting board to this measurement.

Note: If you do not own a table saw, have the board cut at a home center.

2. Cut the fabric to a length that is 2½ times the width of the window; cut the fabric in half lengthwise. (Set the other half aside to use for a matching valance on another window or for another project.) Using the fusible hem tape and following the manufacturer's directions, hem the edges of the fabric.

3. Fold the fabric to find the center; staple the top edge of the fabric center to the back edge of the board center. Pull the fabric taut from the center. Staple the top edge of the fabric along the back edge of the board at 1-inch intervals; allow the fabric "tails" to hang freely.

4. To mount the treatment, screw the board to the trim above the window. At each top corner of the window, tie a large, loose knot in the fabric and allow the fabric "tails" to hang down the sides of the window.

5. Determine the width to cut the swag fabric, and add 1 inch for ½-inch seam allowances. For the length, measure the drop (from the drapery rod to approximately the middle of the window side); multiply by 2, then add the drapery rod measurement, plus 1 inch.

6. Cut the fabric and a lining fabric to these measurements.

7. Sew the fabric pieces together, leaving an opening for turning. Clip the corners, turn right side out, and press. Sew the opening closed.

8. Mount the rod above the window and drape the swag from the rod.

BOX-PLEAT VALANCE

Materials
54-inch-wide decorator fabric for valance and top cover
54-inch-wide decorator fabric for pleats
Lining fabric
Straight pins
Iron and ironing board
Sewing thread in matching colors
½-inch-thick mounting board
Staple gun, staples
L-brackets, screwdriver, screws

Step by Step

1. Determine the finished width of the valance based on where it will be mounted outside the window trim. Determine the amount of the return (the distance from the wall to the front of the valance) needed to clear the window trim and any hardware mounted behind the valance.

2. Determine the number of inverted pleats you would like to have across the finished width of the valance, spacing them equally. (Typical spacing is 6 to 10 inches apart.) Do not include returns when you are figuring the number of pleats.

3. Determine the size to cut the valance fabric. (Length = desired finished length + 2½ inches. Width = desired finished width + returns + 4 inches for side hems + 5 inches for each pleat.) Cut decorator fabric to these measurements. If the valance is wider than the fabric, sew fabric lengths together, matching patterns as needed, to achieve the desired width.

4. Determine the placement of the first pleat by measuring in from one edge of the valance the depth of the return, plus 2 inches for the side hem; also add the amount of space allowed between each set of pleats. Measure 2½ inches on each side of the spot, and mark vertical lines down the fabric length with straight pins at these marks. These pin lines mark the folds of the first pleat. Repeat this measuring and pinning process from the other edge of the valance to mark the other outer pleat. To mark the remaining pleats, measure the determined space between pleats from the center of one marked pleat to the center of the next, then mark with pins 2½ inches from each side of the pleats' centers.

5. For contrasting pleats, cut a piece of pleat fabric 5 inches wide and the length of the valance fabric; repeat for each pleat. Cut the valance fabric apart vertically down the center of each 5-inch-wide marked pleat.

6. With right sides together and matching raw edges, position a piece of pleat fabric on the valance fabric along the first cut edge for the first pleat; sew, and press seam allowances toward the valance fabric. Align the other edge of the pleat fabric with the second cut edge of the valance fabric for the first pleat; sew, and press seam allowances toward the valance fabric. Repeat to secure each piece of pleat fabric to each pleat cut in the valance fabric. This positions the contrasting fabric inside the inverted pleats.

7. Determine the size to cut the lining fabric. (Length = length of the sewn valance fabric minus 1 inch. Width = width of the sewn valance fabric minus 4 inches.)

8. Cut the lining. Position it on the valance with right sides together, lining up the bottom raw edges and centering lining fabric across the width of the valance (2 inches from each edge). Sew along bottom, open flat, and press seam allowance toward lining fabric. Turn the lining fabric to wrong side of valance and match raw edge to top raw edge of valance; pin in place, folding valance front to back along bottom. Press the bottom folded edge to form hem. Turn under each raw edge of valance front 1 inch twice to form side hems, enclosing the lining's raw edge; press and sew.

9. Bring pinned lines on the front of the valance together to the center of each pleat fabric to form each inverted pleat; pin in place. For creased pleats, pin the pleat at the hem also. Baste the upper edge of the valance together to secure the valance fabric, lining, and pleats together. Press pleats in place.

10. Cut a piece of wood as long as the width of the finished valance and as wide as the determined valance-return measurement. This piece will be mounted parallel to the ceiling, like a shelf above the window.

11. Determine the size to cut the valance cover piece. (Length = length of the wood + 1½ inches. Width = width of the wood + 1 inch.) Cut cover piece. Turn under one long edge of fabric ½ inch twice; sew. Mark the center of the other long edge. Position the valance on the cover piece with right sides together, lining up the top of the valance with the long raw edge of the cover piece and matching the center points. Pin the valance to the three unhemmed edges of the cover pieces, turning corners and easing the fit to line up the valance ends with the hemmed edge of the cover piece. Sew, pivoting fabric at corners. Clip corners for a smooth fit. Turn right side out.

12. Position valance on the wood with the cover over the top of the wood and the valance hanging from the front edge of the wood; staple through the fabric to secure. Mount with L-brackets.

Better Homes and Gardens·
Creative Collection™

Editorial Director John Riha

Editor in Chief Deborah Gore Ohrn

Executive Editor Karman Wittry Hotchkiss

Managing Editor Kathleen Armentrout

Contributing Editorial Manager Heidi Palkovic

Contributing Design Director Tracy DeVenney

Contributing Editor Becky Mollenkamp
Copy Chief Mary Heaton
Contributing Copy Editor Mary Helen Schiltz
Proofreader Joleen Ross
Administrative Assistant Lori Eggers

Publishing Group President
Jack Griffin

President and CEO Stephen M. Lacy

Chairman of the Board William T. Kerr

In Memoriam
E. T. Meredith III (1933–2003)